To the Extreme

Wakeboarding

by Christine Peterson

Reading Consultant:
Barbara J. Fox
Reading Specialist
North Carolina State University

Capstone press

Mankato, Minnesota

Blazers is published by Capstone Press,
151 Good Counsel Drive, P.O. Box 669, Mankato, Minnesota 56002.
www.capstonepress.com

Library of Congress Cataloging-in-Publication Data
Peterson, Christine, 1961–
    Wakeboarding / by Christine Peterson.
    p. cm.—(Blazers—to the extreme)
    Includes bibliographical references and index.
    ISBN 0-7368-3788-4 (hardcover)
    1. Wakeboarding—Juvenile literature. I. Title. II. Series.
GV840.W34P48 2005
797.3—dc22   2004016619

Summary: Describes the sport of wakeboarding, including tricks and
    safety information.

Credits
Jason Knudson, set designer; Enoch Peterson, book designer;
    Scott Thoms, photo editor; Kelly Garvin, photo researcher

Photo Credits
Getty Images Inc./Chris McGrath, 25
Rick Doyle, cover, 5, 6, 7, 8, 11, 12, 13, 15, 16–17, 19, 20, 22,
    22–23, 23, 27, 28–29
SportsChrome Inc./Sport the Library/Adam Dodd, 21; Brett
    Stanley, 5 (inset)

**Capstone Press thanks Scott Atkinson, director of communications,
USA Water Ski, Polk City, Florida, for his contributions to this book.**

1 2 3 4 5 6 10 09 08 07 06 05

Table of Contents

Catching Air

A wakeboarder pops off a large wake behind a motorboat. He sails above the water. He aims his wakeboard toward the sky.

He spins upside down as the board sails over his head. The wakeboarder flips around in the air.

The wakeboarder lands with a splash. He has performed an aerial front flip. Now he zips across the lake to try another trick.

BLAZER FACT

Wakeboarders "stomp" a trick when they land smoothly in the water.

Wakeboards

Motorboats pull wakeboarders across lakes and rivers. Wakeboarders perform tricks on the wakes behind the boats.

Wake

Wakeboarders hold onto towropes. The towrope hooks to the boat. Wakeboards have fins. Fins help wakeboarders steer.

Towrope

BLAZER FACT

Boats often carry weights called "fat sacks" to make larger wakes.

Fin

13

Wakeboards are part surfboard and part water ski. Wakeboards are curved to get lift. Bindings hold wakeboarders' feet to their boards.

BLAZER FACT

"Skurfers" were the first wakeboards. Skurfers looked like surfboards.

Wakeboarder Diagram

Wet suit

Towrope handle

Bindings

Fin

Tricks

Wakeboarders fly through the air
to perform aerial grabs. They hold
the towrope with one hand. They
reach back to grab their boards.

Wakeboarders do grab moves. They touch the sides or ends of their boards. For some grabs, wakeboarders turn upside down.

21

Wakeboarders push off from wakes to do inverts. They fly into the air. Wakeboarders spin backward to grab their boards.

safety

Wakeboarders know how to stay safe. They wear life vests. Some wakeboarders also wear helmets when they perform tricks.

Most wakeboarders are good swimmers. They know how to safely fall in wipeouts. After falls, they are ready to ride more wakes.

Catching big air

Glossary

aerial (AIR-ee-uhl)—a trick performed in the air

bindings (BINE-dingz)—the shoelike parts that hold a rider's feet to the board

fin (FIN)—a small metal piece on the bottom of a wakeboard to help with steering

invert (in-VURT)—a trick performed upside down in the air

towrope (TOE-rohp)—the rope a wakeboarder hangs onto while being pulled behind a motorboat; the towrope is attached to the motorboat.

wake (WAYK)—the V-shaped trail of waves left behind a moving boat

wipeout (WIPE-out)—a fall or crash

Read More

Blomquist, Christopher. *Wakeboarding in the X Games*. Kids' Guide to the X Games. New York: PowerKids Press, 2003.

Maurer, Tracy Nelson. *Wakeboarding*. Radsports Guides. Vero Beach, Fla.: Rourke, 2003.

Schaefer, A.R. *Extreme Wakeboarding Moves*. Behind the Moves. Mankato, Minn.: Capstone Press, 2003.

Internet Sites

FactHound offers a safe, fun way to find Internet sites related to this book. All of the sites on FactHound have been researched by our staff.

Here's how:

1. Visit *www.facthound.com*
2. Type in this special code **0736837884** for age-appropriate sites. Or enter a search word related to this book for a more general search.
3. Click on the **Fetch It** button.

FactHound will fetch the best sites for you!

Index